lessons from my lunchbox

lessons from my Lunchbox

Overcoming the bullies one note at a time

Rachel Chadima

two harbors press — minneapolis, mn

Two Harbors Press
322 First Avenue N, 5th floor
Minneapolis, MN 55401
612.455.2293
www.TwoHarborsPress.com

ISBN-13: 978-1-63413-958-8
LCCN: 2015921274

Distributed by Itasca Books
Cover and note design by Sara Schultz www.saraschultz.co
Photos by Rachel Seifert www.rachabellaphotography.com
Author Website: www.lessonsfrommylunchbox.com
Typeset by B. Cook

Printed in the United States of America

This book is dedicated to:

A woman of faith, love, patience, kindness, selflessness, strength, and grace—Mom, I admire you in every way. Thank you for your endless love and support, and for lighting my path through your love and God's word. This one's for you!

Dad, thank you for always being there for me and for being my biggest cheerleader. A man of true integrity, loyalty, and generosity—you have a heart of gold. I'm forever grateful for your guidance, love, and advice, and I'm proud to call you mine.

To my angels, then and now, thank you for carrying me sweetly on your wings of support, love, and encouragement. I love you all!

Turning Life's Storms into Sunshine

At an early age, I found my passion for motivating, teaching, and helping others to be their very best. Whether sharing my love for dance through performing and teaching, cheering on my family and friends as they journey through life, leading students through yoga classes, or helping women find an outfit they love, I feel most at home when uplifting others. So, when I graduated from the University of St. Thomas with my degree in Public Relations and Family Studies in 2011, I felt incredibly fortunate to jump into a career at CorePower Yoga where I had the opportunity to uplift and inspire my students and teachers every day. I was on cloud nine, but the world outside of the yoga studio was in need of a little TLC—an important matter was at hand:

Bullying.

The heart-wrenching problem had not only gained attention from the media, schools, and parents across the globe, but it was especially hitting close to home—in me. I knew I had to do something to help.

That's when God put into my heart the dream of writing a book about my experience overcoming the mean girls and the bullies.

Scary? YES! But, as Joel Osteen says: "Make your mess your message." So I took a leap of faith. I trusted that by sharing my story and my mom's sweet notes with the world, I could make a difference.

And so it began.

As I sat behind my computer late at night in the house that built me, at the kitchen table that held years of memories, I started to pour my heart out in my story, and I could feel God working through me. He was there through every tear-filled sentence that I wrote about my school days, and every smile on my face as I read through thirteen years' worth of my mom's lunchbox notes that I had saved throughout my life.

I prayed and prayed that each word I wrote would be a blessing to someone—that my words would provide them with hope and confidence, and would be a reminder that they are loved—"BIG time"—just as my mom and dad always reminded me with the notes Mom left in my lunchbox. And, after endless edits, hours, proofreads, and seasons spent at that kitchen table, here I am with a book in my hands—my dream has come true!

I wrote *Lessons from My Lunchbox* with one goal, one hope, and one prayer: that my story—and my mom's notes—would uplift you, inspire you, and give you hope.

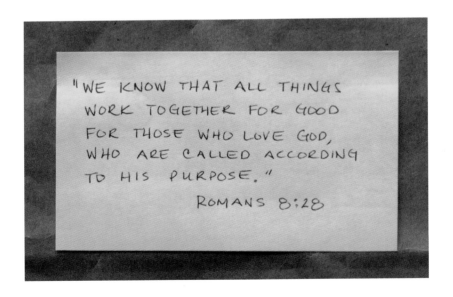

That simple verse was one of my favorite pieces of Scripture to read on the lunchbox notes I received from my mom. It couldn't be more true. God really has used all of my challenges and experiences for good—to help me grow and help others—and he can use your challenges for good, too!

So, to the PB&J-spreadin', Mac and Cheese-makin', lunch-packin' moms and dads out there, this one's for you and yours! I pray that my story and my mom's sweet notes will give you and your loved ones the hope and encouragement to shine, dance, sing, and smile through every one of life's "bullystorms."

From my lunchbox to yours,

Rachel

Rachel—
Dad and I are
so lucky to
have a kid like
you!!

Rachel— One of
my greatest joys
in life is having
you for my
daughter and my
♡ is filled
everyday by the
love we have for
one another
love you, mom

O GIVE THANKS TO THE
LORD,
FOR HE IS GOOD; HIS

STEADFAST love ENDURES
FOREVER!

PSALM 118:1

RACHEL,
YOU ARE PRECIOUS
TO US!
HUGS,
MOM & DAD

... For truly I tell you, if you
have faith the size of a
mustard seed, you will say
to this mountain, move from here
to there, and it will move; and
nothing will be impossible
for you.
Matthew 17:20

LIFE IS A JOURNEY
FULL OF ADVENTURE.
SMILE, ASK
QUESTIONS, LOOK
FOR THE GOOD IN
EVERY THING, DRINK
LOTS OF WATER, &
WASH YOUR HANDS.
LOVE YOU.

Surround us with your angels, Lord open our eyes to their direction. Open our ears to their whispers. Thank you for sending them to watch over us. Rachel-you are loved.

For God commands the angels to guard you in all your ways. Psalm 91:11

Rachel
you are my ray of sunshine
you warm my ♡
love you,
Mom

YOU ARE LOVED . . . . .

BIG

TIME!!

LIFE IS GRAND!
END OF QUARTER

THANK YOUR TEACHERS
ENJOY AND SMILE
JOB WELL DONE!!
GREAT GRADES!
YOU ARE A SMART
YOUNG LADY◇

Special Something
In My Lunchbox

Special Something in My Lunchbox

My lunches were *the ultimate* cold lunches of cold lunches. I'm not talking brown paper bags filled with squished PB&J, and crackers with spray cheese. Think enormous, organic turkey sandwiches sealed with pink Saran Wrap and flower stickers, colorful fruit salads, and veggies complete with homemade dill dip.

Oh! And don't forget about the freshly baked homemade chocolate chip cookies—one for me, and, of course, one for my BFF, Libby.

I always brought cold lunches to school, but a Lunchable never met the inside of my lunchbox unless Dad made a quick stop at the family-owned grocery store on our drive to school just so I could give the ever-so-popular cold marinara a try. One thing's for sure: Lunchable cardboard pizzas may've been all the rage in my elementary school, but they definitely didn't earn you a spot at the cool table in the *high school* cafeteria.

You could draw a map in your wide-ruled notebook of where every clique sat, and heaven forbid you got stuck sitting with the un-athletic, bookworm-fantastic, band geeks at one of the *round* tables. Everyone knew that a seat at one of the round tables could easily rob you of your reputation, and that a damaged reputation was enough for the queen bee of your clique to kick you to the curb.

Within moments of stepping foot into my high school cafeteria and glancing at the hot lunch line, I could always tell which cliques were fighting and who was best friends with whom that week. The only thing worse than standing in the hot lunch line was standing *alone* in the hot lunch line. Standing alone screamed "outsider," and everyone knew that "in" was the only place to be. Staying in the "in crowd," however, was the hardest part.

The odds of doing something "so *not* cool" were higher than doing something "so *totally* cool" in any clique of queen bees and wannabees. A simple game of "she loves me, she loves me not" could drive you from "most popular girl in school" status to sitting at one of the round tables trading Pokémon cards. Chatting about Charizard and Pikachu was *so* fifth grade, and no sophomore wanted to be caught with their old Pokémon card collection.

Luckily, getting demoted to the outcast table was never a worry of Libby's or mine. Unlike the snotty girls with their ever-shifting seats just a few spots down from us, you'd never find Libb and I playing musical chairs; we had been best friends since our first *shuffle-shuffle-hop-step* in dance class when we were three years old, and we knew we'd always be in sync.

She and I always sat next to each other at the cool kids' table where the name-brand food in our lunchboxes was just as cool as having "Abercrombie and Fitch" stitched boldly across the front of our sweatshirts. While the queen bees judged their neighbors' so-last-season Hollister outfit and off-brand fruit snacks at the other end of the table, I shielded my little off-brand yellow lunchbox as I unzipped its three sides. To spare myself weird looks, I cracked the top just enough to sneak out my freshly baked treats. Keeping the lunchbox lid closed was my best tactic for hiding the "birdseed bread" turkey sandwich I loved from the mean girls who made fun of me for eating the "weird" organic bread from the freezer section at the grocery store.

But, it wasn't one of the eighty-six kids in my class taunting me about my organic lunches, or the "Birdseed Bread" song I heard lunch after lunch that got my feet tap dancing anxiously under the table.

There was something special inside my lunchbox, something so special to me that all through high school I played "reach inside and pull out a surprise" to avoid the lid of my lunchbox flying open.

Dessert is always supposed to come first, right?

I feared what could happen if the lid were to open, a spotlight shining brightly inside, and my favorite part of my lunch exposed for all to see. I could only imagine all of my peers pointing and laughing at what I knew my mom so purposefully taped inside my lunchbox every day.

Without a doubt, a small, hand-written note, filled with love and lifelong lessons, was always waiting for me.

Carefully crafted with my mom's love, some notes were long and others shorter. She wrote me a note every day from kindergarten through senior year. It was her way of loving me, encouraging me, and guiding my steps while I was out navigating a world of brats and bullies.

And, believe me, my lunch table was full of them.

So, while the mean girls shared the latest gossip up and down the weathered lunch table, my mom shared encouraging lessons on life through her notes. She reminded me to believe in myself, to work hard, be a true friend, spend time with God, trust His plan, help others, have compassion for the bullies, and follow my heart.

I cherished her every word, but—fearful of the mocking I might receive—I read each one discreetly. (Can you blame me?) No one else's mom was writing them sweet notes during those growing-up years when we all needed them most. Oreos were about as sweet as it got in most lunchboxes, but even though Oreos had a long shelf life, the expiration date on my mom's words read "everlasting."

Each note she left in my lunchbox became a part of my roadmap for overcoming the bullies and mean girls, especially in high school. Her words empowered me to follow my own road— the road *less* traveled—when many of my peers were flying down the road *most* traveled by curious teenagers.

Peer pressure may've been my classmates' co-pilot, but Mom and Dad were my fearless navigators, and my mom's lunchbox notes were my very own GPS.

I knew where I was headed. I had direction, and no one at my lunch table (except for Libb) ever caught a glimpse of one of my secret roadmaps—Mom's notes. After all, after years of wellie-wearin' weather, the last thing I needed was another "bullystorm" rollin' in.

But, who was I kidding?

The bullying had started early—and the rumors only rumbled louder as I grew taller.

RACHEL
Great things about you!
Nice, fun, creative, energetic,
loving, great at piano, dance
and basketball, excellent
explorer and so sweet!
God loves you and so do we.
Mom & Dad

Smile, choose an
attitude of
Enthusiasm! always
remember, you are a
treasure.
hugs and love

Rachel, you are a
little flower, that
we love to watch
grow ♡
hugs and love

RACHEL, DAD & I
LOVE HAVING YOU
FOR OUR DAUGHTER
AND WE LOVE ALL
THE TIME WE
SPEND TOGETHER ♡
KNOW YOU ARE LOVED
* FRESH COOKIES
WHEN I PICK YOU
UP FROM SCHOOL!
HUGS, MOM & DAD

RC
MOVE THROUGH THE
DAY WITH...
STRENGTH ✓
OPTIMISM ✓
FAITH ✓
HOPE ✓
LOVE YOU SWEET GIRL

Life is a journey ~ full of adventure, smile, ask questions, look for fun in everything, drink lots of water and wash your hands. Love you!

RACHEL, YOU ARE A CAN DO GIRL. LOVED BY MANY. WITH 2 HUGS AND 2 KISSES WE LOVE YOU!

Rachel, you are respectful and responsible
A   you are adored by mom & dad
C   You are caring and creative
H   you are a great helper
E   you are an exceptional speller
L   you are loved

TOBIE WILL SMILE WHEN YOU GET HOME TODAY AND WHISKERS WILL BE PURRING WHEN YOU WALK IN THE BARN..
WOOF! WOOF!

Small Town Bullystorms

Small Town Bullystorms

The small town I grew up in wasn't for the faint of heart. You were either in the townie circle or you were out. And, unless your last name sat somewhere between your aunts', grandparents', cousins', and fourth cousins' in the slender, twelve-page phone book, most likely you were out. Without extended family down the road, I figured out pretty quickly that no closet full of raincoats and wellies would help me weather the small town gossip storms.

Who are the out-of-towners? That question greeted my parents when they moved from the concrete jungle to the land of green acres to pursue my dad's dream of farming. True believers in hard work, Mom and Dad built their American dream on the 1,200-acre farm I grew up on, and, as the crops grew, curiosity amongst the locals did, too.

It wasn't long before the flood warning for chatter started flashing in our everyone-knows-everything small town, and like the branded cows roaming the farm, we were branded "out-of-towners" even before I was running through the open fields. Small towns gossip—and they don't talk quietly when they do—so as soon as the locals tracked my family's ties to the famous golden arches and Big Mac, the story behind my last name was supersized.

Absolutely supersized.

In kindergarten, my classmates started collecting rumors about my close-knit family like other children collected Happy Meal toys. They heard stories from their parents—who had heard stories from their neighbor's neighbors at the hardware store—and they weren't afraid to spread them across the seats of the yellow school bus.

The wheels on the bus weren't the only things that went round and round.

"Rachel has servants and a McDonald's kitchen in her house," they yelled as I ran off of the school bus into my mom's loving arms; my heart pounding through my floral backpack as tears raced down my cheeks.

The rumors and snickers that echoed through the bus's windows at the bus stop sent my parents into bully-proofing mode. Quickly. And it all started during my mom's morning devotions with a pen, a Post-it note, her Bible, and a whole lotta love.

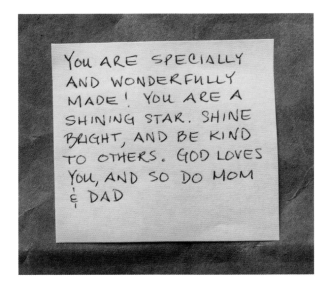

That note peeked through the tiny opening of my lunchbox as I lifted the lid on the school bus one morning—some days I just couldn't wait until lunch to see what my mom had written me. Reading Mom's sweet words made sitting alone and enduring the spitball wars just a little easier. But, those spitballs stuck in my hair day after day? Enough was enough.

In first grade, I traded in the spitball-flyin', "no-room-for-you"-taunting school bus rides once and for all for a seat next to Dad on what we called "The Red Bus." With air conditioning, Aerosmith playing through the speakers, and someone to practice my spelling words with—his red Chevy pickup truck was a total upgrade. Plus, I loved being with my dad.

I was fascinated by his passion for the land, his drive, his big heart, and his kind way with people. I studied his boot prints in the soil like most kids watched the Disney channel—with tunnel vision—and learned so much from his work ethic and integrity. Every day during chores, my black lab, Tobie, and I followed him around the beautiful farm that my bare feet loved even more than my favorite pair of sparkly shoes. (And I really, *really* loved my sparkly red shoes.)

I wasn't your typical farm girl. Bib overalls weren't my first choice for sitting in the cab of Dad's tractor. Vintage dresses from the dress-up trunk and fresh daisy-flower crowns, made by Mom's loving hands, were my everyday uniform for feeding the baby calves and exploring the hay fields. I believed grandma's vintage dresses were even more beautiful with a little dirt on the hem from running through the open fields that I felt lucky enough to call "home sweet home."

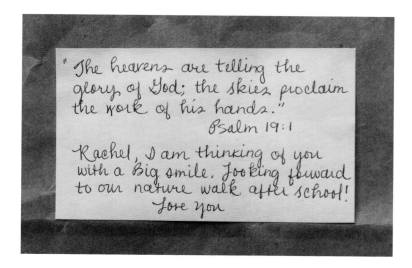

This is one of my favorite notes from elementary school. Freedom to explore and put down roots in those acres was every little kid's dream, and being out in nature gave me a strong appreciation for God's creation.

Everything about my upbringing was magical: Mom and Dad showered me with love, and they taught me to put my faith and hope in God. My best friends were like sisters to me, and I had beautiful green fields to roam. Exploring those, I discovered who I was at my core.

Mom's notes reminded me of that center on the days when girls circled me on the playground, quizzing me about the rumors they had heard on the school bus.

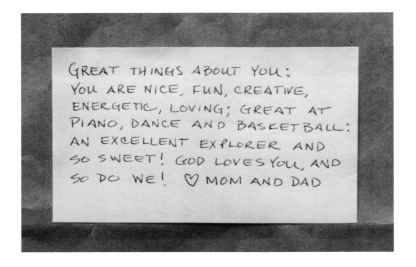

Her notes helped me keep my head up while the girls pulled my braided pigtails down and taunted me for riding to school with Dad. No matter how many times those girls kicked dirt at me during a game of recess kickball, I knew from Mom's notes that I was loved.

Big time!

As I grew older, sweet and simple notes saying "I love you" turned into more complex notes telling me "You're capable and so strong." Riding horses with mom through the rolling hills of our farm gave way to covering textbooks with shopping bags and decorating my first locker. Sleepovers that ended with Dad coming to pick me up because the lemon drop "homesick pills" didn't work gave way to coed parties where the boys and girls were too shy to even look at each other. Colorful Lisa Frank folders were all replaced with a single, more studious, Trapper Keeper.

Groups of undeniable friends faded away and became an endless fight to find your place. Growing up changed to growing out—in all new places. And sweet elementary-school days gave way to sassy middle-school days.

Bring on the rainbow-colored braces!

Whatever your talent is, it is of God. If it's something that makes your heart sing... that's God's way of telling you it's a contribution he wants you to make.

— Marianne Williamson
Return to Love

WE HAVE GIFTS THAT DIFFER ACCORDING TO THE GRACE GIVEN TO US... ROMANS 12:6

Rachel
you are a treasure and you are loved
xo Mom & Dad

RACHEL, KNOW YOU ARE HERE WITH A PURPOSE, MADE WITH PURE LOVE ♡ WORK HARD AT WHAT YOU LOVE TO DO!
GOD LOVES YOU AND SO DO WE ♡

RACHEL, ALL YOUR FRIENDS HAVE DIFFERENT GIFTS AND YOU HAVE FOUND ONE OF YOUR MANY. IT IS YOURS TO SHARE WITH HUMILITY AND PASSION.
HAVE A NICE DAY!
XO MOM

Rachel
It is your time to shine you made it happen. Enjoy the moment and thank God for your many talents!!
Love you!

.. LET YOUR LIGHT SHINE BEFORE OTHERS, SO THAT THEY MAY SEE YOUR GOOD WORKS AND GIVE GLORY TO YOUR FATHER IN HEAVEN.   MATTHEW 5:16
RACHEL YOU ARE GIFTED, KIND AND LOVED!!

friends are kind to each others hopes. they cherish each others dreams
— henry david thoreau
rachel—
Keep being the sweet girl you are.

Rachel,
You are the star in your mom & Dads eyes. Kind, intelligent, loving and beautiful. You amaze us! Chase your dreams ♡
Love You

Rachel ⟶ you are an inspiration to me. It was amazing and delightful to watch you dance this past weekend. A Joy! You shine with Beauty, Class and Grace!
Love You

Rachel, Let your light shine no matter who rolls their eyes with jealousy from the Sidelines. Believe in yourself!! Hugs & Love

I have strength for everything through him who empowers me. Philippians 4:13
Congrats honey! You did it! We are so proud of you ♡ Thinking of you with a smile!!

Crimped Hair, Braces
And
The Teenage Identity Crisis

Crimped Hair, Braces, and the Teenage Identity Crisis

"Where do I belong?" "Does he like me?" "What am I good at?" These were the kinds of questions running through our hormonal middle-school minds. Boys didn't know that roughhousing wasn't a "cute" way of showing us girls that they had a crush on us, and sassy seemed to be the latest trend among the girls.

Preteen moods were just like the fashion trends—always changing—and time spent with Dad during our drives to school changed as I got older, too.

Our eight-minute spelling bees turned into eight-minute pep talks. He shared loving advice about overcoming the bullies, staying true to myself, being kind, and encouraging my peers. And, just before dropping me off at the front doors of my middle school, he always reminded me that I was a treasure—no matter which sixth-grade boy tried to tell me that treasures only came at the bottom of the Cap'n Crunch box. What did sixth-grade boys know, anyway?

Notes saying,

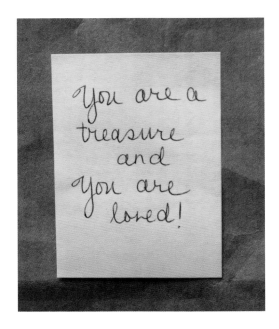

lit up my lunchbox frequently, and always made me smile.

To me, treasures weren't those plastic toys in cereal boxes; treasures were Mom's notes in my lunchbox.

Even before stepping foot in the bustling hallways, I always wondered what my mom had written that day to guide me through the drama, mood swings, and all-consuming search for my place in the circle of sassiness. I'd clutch my lunchbox on the drive to school as if it were the season's brand new Jansport backpack, bracing myself for the latest episode of my middle-school soap opera as I watched cornfields pass in the rearview mirror. My lunchbox may not have looked as fabulous as a must-have backpack from the outside, but I knew the real treasure was inside.

My parents' love and Mom's daily notes had been my constants since kindergarten and, in middle school, I needed them more than ever.

The teenage identity crisis was in full swing and jealousy was the star of the show. With high school just around the corner, everyone's biggest fear was being "the blender"—the so-so talent of the school. Dancer, football stud, honor roll student, state-champion runner, concert pianist, scouted baseball player—everyone was searching for their starring niche.

Everyone—except for me.

I had fallen in love with dance when I was three years old, and my parents had done all they could to fuel my passion. After hundreds of dinners in the back seat, thousands of miles put on the Suburban, and years of Mom driving me to and from the dance studio, I was one of the first in my class to come into my own.

My heart was singing.

Even as a fourteen-year-old, I knew I had found something special, and I couldn't wait to share my passion and perform a dance solo for the first time in front of my friends and peers at the middle school talent show.

read the note Dad had snuck into my lunchbox that morning; I repeated his words in my head as I walked onto the performance floor in front of the entire school. My adrenaline pumped as I floated across the old gym floor with grace, and when I hit my final pose, I knew from Libby's cheers and applause that I had hit that solo performance out of the park. But, I got a feeling from a few of the girls' faces in the audience that they weren't as thrilled about my home run as Libb was.

And, boy, was I right!

They realized that I had already found my niche, and I could hear their isolating bully showers rollin' in the moment I took my bow.

Now the girl who pushed me down on the playground when I was little wouldn't let me join "her" circle in the middle-school hallways. This was absolutely, positively, most definitely the worst sign that now I was the girl on the outside. I was living the nightmare you read in every girls' diary.

Uncovering what I loved and sharing it with all my peers suddenly made me stand out, the one who was not quite like the rest, the one who . . . yup . . . "didn't fit in."

Most of the girls I had called friends couldn't handle that the spotlight was on me, instead of them, and their desire for attention fluffed up bigger than their crimped hair. It only got bigger as our grade numbers did. Before long, their attitudes were as big as the platform Sketchers on their feet, and they went out of their way to try to walk all over me.

A spot at the lunch table was now "invite only." They'd glare at me and whisper to each other as they passed notes back and forth in science class. The girls in my locker bay belittled the awards I won at dance competitions so much that other mean girls chimed in.

I would bury my head in my locker, pretending to dig for something in my backpack, just so they wouldn't see the tears in my eyes.

I never imagined the busy middle school hallways could feel so lonely. But, through the tears, Mom and Dad made sure that I kept pursuing what I loved, no matter who rolled their eyes from the sidelines.

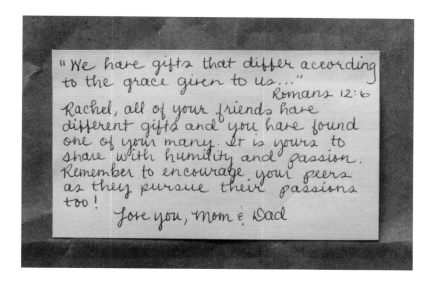

"We have gifts that differ according to the grace given to us..."
Romans 12:6
Rachel, all of your friends have different gifts and you have found one of your many. It is yours to share with humility and passion. Remember to encourage your peers as they pursue their passions too!
Love you, Mom & Dad

Unfortunately, eyes weren't the only things rolling. The boat my girlfriends and I had sailed since kindergarten rocked from the rolling waves of unease and jealousy as we sailed towards our first day of high school. Sure footing had changed as quickly as training bra sizes, and Libb and I were the only two getting seasick. *Dramamine, anyone?!*

From the way our days were tossed, she and I started to wonder if we should pull out the life vests. Would our group of girlfriends make it?

We knew we had to do something.

Since CliffsNotes didn't publish *How to Prepare for High School*, Libb and I decided to create a promise, like the girls in the *Sisterhood of the Traveling Pants* had done, with hopes of it preserving our group of girlfriends as we sailed into what would become the perfect storm.

Since a pair of magical, one-size-fits-all traveling jeans only existed in the movies, we decided to each wear a thin gold ring to remind us of the promise we'd make.

"No drinking, sex, or drugs through high school" was what we promised each other. How long did that last? Well, for some it immediately looked like rough seas ahead, but I was bound and determined to hold true to the promise I made—and to help all of my girlfriends do the same.

Besides, our group of girlfriends was as close as the Spice Girls, and—if you asked us—the Spice Girls were going to last forever.

And, so would we.

Do not be conformed to this world, but be transformed by the renewal of your mind that you may discern what is the will of God, what is good, pleasing and perfect
Romans 12:2

RACHEL,
THE CREAM ALWAYS
RISES TO THE TOP!
AND
YOU'RE THE CREAM!
VISUALIZE
YOUR DREAMS COMING
TRUE.
YOU ARE LOVED
MOM & DAD

Rachel,
I see you dancing in my minds eye, bringing forth Energy, Passion and Control, Beauty and Grace... moving across the old wood floor.
The vision makes us smile
Love you, MOM & DAD

Rachel → You are wonderfully made, unlike anyone else. Embrace your unique qualities and continue to use them to help and inspire others.

You are wonderfully made, Unlike anyone else. Embrace your unique qualities and continue to use them to help and inspire others. Thinking of you with a smile.

dare to be different and stay true to yourself. no one ever made an impact on the world without standing out from crowd, so embrace your unique qualities. They are what makes you unforgettable!
(Gail Blanke)

Visualize
See yourself achieving
your goal.

Rachel—
Let your light shine
and
Wow the crowd!!
Love you,
Mom & Dad

... LET YOUR GOOD
SPIRIT LEAD ME
ON A LEVEL
PATH.
PSALM 143:10

RACHEL,
STAY TRUE TO
WHAT YOU KNOW
TO BE RIGHT. WE
TRUST YOU TO MAKE
GOOD DECISIONS.
LOVE YOU

I will instruct you and teach
you the way you should go; I
will counsel you with my eye
upon you.   Psalm 32:8
Rachel, High school has arrived!
Stay on your level road and true
to what you know is right.
Push yourself to do well. Enjoy the
new people & opportunities. You can
do whatever you put your mind to. ♡

RACHEL,
YOU WILL NEVER
REGRET BEING THE
NICE, KIND PERSON
YOU ARE
INSIDE & OUT!
LOVE YOU

6 Pack? You mean...
Of Sprite?

Six-pack? You Mean . . . of Sprite?

Not so fast, Sporty Spice! Boys, alcohol, peer pressure, parties, catty girls, cliques, and the fight to fit in were all in the forecast, and, boy, did it rain.

Hard.

The moment I stepped foot in the high school hallways, I could see how easy it was to be pulled into what everyone else was doing, which was nothing great: drugs, alcohol, sex, crash dieting—all the "age appropriate" hobbies for young adults, thanks to MTV.

Now the party you attended over the weekend—and the upperclassman's car you rode shotgun in—were way cooler than the sleepover you had with your BFFs. And the passenger seat wasn't the only thing freshman girls were shot-gunning.

"Shot-gunning" beer at parties had become an all-time favorite extracurricular, but the invite to a party in the senior basketball star's parents' basement—which some of our classmates considered a dream come true—wasn't on Libby's or my vision board. We knew that partaking in any behavior seen on MTV's *The Real World* wouldn't go over so well with our parents. We also knew that we were living in the *real*, real world, where the intentions of upper-class boys were questionable.

But, for most high school girls, boys' intentions didn't matter as much as their attention did, and they were shopping the attention and validation aisle just like the upper-class boys were shopping the new crop of freshman girls—us!

I knew the promises made by some of these boys were empty, but some of my girlfriends were drooling over every word. Upperclassmen became the only topic of their conversations, and as time went on, their talk at the lunch table belonged in my world less than a Little Debbie snack cake belonged in my lunchbox.

While they were eating up each other's gossip, I was enjoying Mom's words of wisdom.

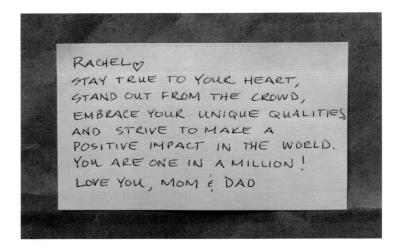

While my classmates were crash dieting and obsessing over their looks, Mom's notes gave me the courage to follow my heart and be confident in my own skin.

While they one-upped each other with how many bases they'd run with their latest crush, I read:

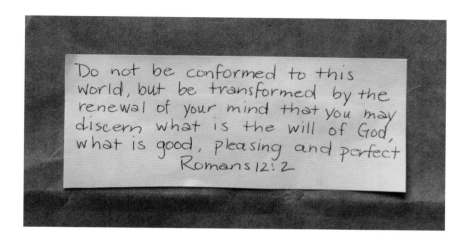

When they started slacking off at practice and made fun of me for working so hard at dance, my passion, my mom encouraged me to:

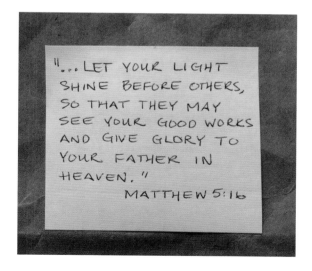

When they started ditching out on plans, making fun of the "unpopular" girls sitting at the round tables, and spreading rumors about the girls they called their "friends" just to gain attention, I read:

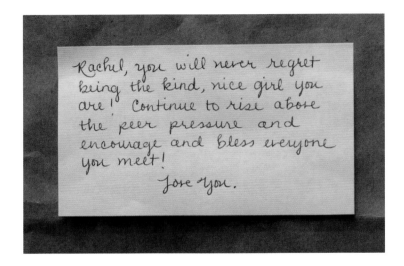

Rachel, you will never regret being the kind, nice girl you are! Continue to rise above the peer pressure and encourage and bless everyone you meet!

Love you.

This was stuff with real value. But, some of my girlfriends' values seemed to be changing quicker than high school relationships.

And that was fast!

They had jumped on the party bus with the rest of our classmates who thought bringing the six-pack to the party would net them popularity. And no, they weren't carrying a six-pack of Sprite . . .

No matter how hard Libb and I tried to keep the band together, our friends were out partying like rock stars—and it looked like their tour had only just begun.

WHAT IS DESIREABLE
IN A PERSON IS LOYALTY.
— PROVERBS 19:22

RACHEL— YOU ARE A GIVING
AND LOVING FRIEND. CONTINUE
ON WITH STRENGTH, HOPE
AND CONFIDENCE.
        XO MOM

THE TESTING OF YOUR
FAITH PRODUCES
PATIENCE. JAMES 1:3

RACHEL, FAITH IS TRUST
AND CONFIDENCE IN
GOD'S TRUTH.
PATIENCE IS A GOOD
THING *
LOVE YOU!

Rachel~ Believe in yourself,
smile, persevere, expect something
good to happen, do what you
love to do, enjoy the moment and
continue to walk with a humble
heart willing to help others
as you always do.
        Love you honey.

Do not worry about anything,
but in everything by prayer and
supplication with Thanksgiving
let your requests be made known
to God. And the peace of God,
which surpasses all understanding
will guard your hearts and minds
in Christ Jesus.
        Philippians 4:6-7

Be strong and courageous!
Do not be frightened or
dismayed, for the Lord, your
God is with you wherever
you go.   Joshua 1:9
Rachel~ Keep your head up.
This too shall pass and the truth
will come out.
        We love you ♡

Rejoice always, pray without
ceasing, give thanks in all
circumstances; for this is
the will of God in Christ
Jesus for you.
        1 Thessalonians 5:16-18

With gratitude and love
but God first. Believe
he has a plan for your
life ∴ :)
Know you are loved.

Rachel → We are proud of
how you have navigated all
your school years thus far :)
Keep your high standards,
ambition, sweet playful spirit,
kind and caring ways.
You are such a good role model!
Have a fabulous day. Hugs ♡

RACHEL, RELEASE
ANY NEGATIVES.
LOOK FORWARD
WITH STRENGTH,
OPTIMISM, ENERGY
AND HOPE !!
GOD LOVES YOU
AND SO DO WE ♡

.. I am with you always even to
the end of the age.
         Matthew 28:20

R♡, no matter what trials we face,
christ never leaves us. He is with
us every step of the way! Even
when you feel alone.
         Love You !

SOME FRIENDS PLAY
AT FRIENDSHIP,
BUT A TRUE FRIEND
STICKS CLOSER THAN
ONE'S NEAREST KIN.
PROVERBS 18:24

The New York Times
Best Sell-Out List

The New York Times Best Sell-Out List

Bullying, spreading rumors, gossiping . . . It seemed that my "friends" were hungry to rule the school. Nothing they were doing aligned with my values, and I couldn't bring myself to crack open a beer, grab a seat on the party bus next to them, and drink down their gossip about our classmates.

After all, word in a small town spreads like wildfire, even in the pouring rain, and I wasn't interested in being front-page news in the local paper. Being labeled "mean girl" or getting an underage drinking ticket wasn't anywhere in my hopes and dreams journal, and neither was running through the woods trying to get away from the cops.

Some of my girlfriends, though, sure put some miles and mud on their party shoes. They had given in to peer pressure in the same way that many girls give in to chocolate, potato chips, and ice cream during *that* time of the month. Not only had my old friends broken our promise, but their gold rings were nowhere in sight. I was crushed.

So crushed.

My old friends had jumped to number one on the *New York Times* Best Sell-Out list right before my eyes, and they completely turned on me. After years of being inseparable, suddenly, we couldn't have been further apart.

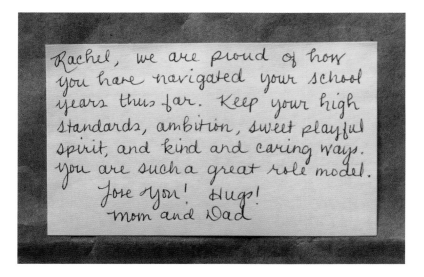

"WHAT IS DESIRABLE IN A PERSON IS LOYALTY..." PROVERBS 19:22 RACHEL, YOU ARE A GIVING AND LOVING FRIEND. CONTINUE ON WITH STRENGTH, HOPE, AND KINDNESS. THANK GOD FOR THE SWEET PEOPLE IN YOUR LIFE AND LET THE OTHERS GO. LOVE YOU, MOM & DAD

While my classmates were writing the headlines in the *Gossip Times*, Mom's lunchbox notes helped me keep my head up and follow the path my heart knew to be right and true.

Rachel, we are proud of how you have navigated your school years thus far. Keep your high standards, ambition, sweet playful spirit, and kind and caring ways. You are such a great role model. Love you! Hugs! Mom and Dad

I wasn't going to let anyone get in my way as I walked that path—even though my old BFFs tried. Nothing bothered my old friends more than seeing me stay true to my values and taste buds while they searched for themselves in the latest fad and at the bottom of a beer can. As they watched me travel the straight and narrow—live out my faith, work hard in school, develop my passions, uphold the gold ring promise and share it with other classmates, nurture my unbreakable friendship with Libb, and stick up for our classmates they bullied—they realized they had taken a wrong turn.

They wanted nothing more than to watch me falter with them.

They couldn't take it.

Middle-school jealousies had grown into a funnel cloud hovering above me on the high-school weather radar. My old friends' envy turned that funnel cloud into a tornado touchdown.

Right in front of me.

"So, I tell you, whatever you ask for in prayer, believe that you have received it and it will be yours."
Mark 11:24

Do not be afraid of them, for I am with you to deliver you, says the Lord.
Jeremiah 1:8

DO NOT THEREFORE ABANDON THAT CONFIDENCE OF YOURS; IT BRINGS GREAT REWARD
HEBREWS 10:35

RACHEL, YOUR SMILE LIGHTS UP A ROOM, CONTINUE TO SHINE BRIGHT!
♡ MOM & DAD

Though I walk in the midst of dangers, you guard my life when my enemies rage. You stretch out your hand; your right hand saves me.
Psalm 138:7

Rachel, don't let the girls jealousy and lies hurt you ♡. Keep your faith and hope in God's plan for you!

BE STRONG AND BOLD; HAVE NO FEAR OR DREAD OF THEM, BECAUSE IT IS THE LORD YOUR GOD WHO GOES WITH YOU; HE WILL NOT FAIL OR FORSAKE YOU.
DEUTERONOMY 31:6

RACHEL, I AM PRAYING YOU THROUGH, TODAY AND ALWAYS!

And after you have suffered for a little while, the God of all grace, who has called you to his eternal glory in Christ, will himself restore, support, strengthen and establish you.
1 Peter 5:10

EVEN THOUGH YOU INTENDED TO DO HARM TO ME, GOD INTENDED IT FOR GOOD...
GENESIS 50:20

FOR I, THE LORD YOUR GOD, HOLD YOUR RIGHT HAND; IT IS I WHO SAY TO YOU, "DO NOT FEAR, I WILL HELP YOU."
ISAIAH 41:13

Rachel— God will help you through! He will heal your heart and your foot.
Know you are loved ♡

You are a strong and caring young lady. A real team player with integrity. and a role model for the girls who look up to you.

Rachel— Move thru the day with poise, confidence and class. You are a fantastic role model!!
Go around anyone who gets in your way.
You are loved

Bloom Where You Are Planted

Bloom Where You Are Planted

Forget about the girl who pushed me down on the playground in grade school. There were new mean girls in town who were out to do damage and fight their way to the top.

Envy had eaten my old girlfriends up whole and spit them out as drama-lovin', rumor-spreadin', queen-bee-dreamin', bully-crazed, self-absorbed, A-list-hopeful, ringleader wannabes. And they came after me like Black Friday shoppers go after a big TV: on a mission, all manners aside.

They didn't care what they had to do to get their hands on one of the few level-headed models left in stock—me! They sat behind me in class so they could trap my long brown hair between their desk and the back of my chair. They excluded me from anything they could—and made sure I knew it. They tried turning classmates against me. They mocked me for wearing my gold ring. They sat front and center at basketball games to try to distract me when I performed with the dance team at halftime.

You name it, they did it.

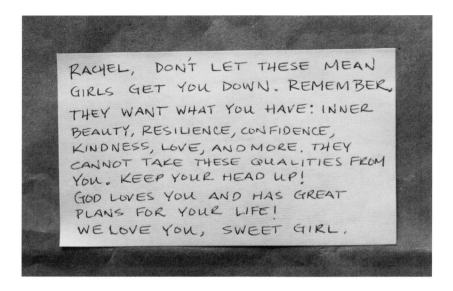

RACHEL, DON'T LET THESE MEAN GIRLS GET YOU DOWN. REMEMBER, THEY WANT WHAT YOU HAVE: INNER BEAUTY, RESILIENCE, CONFIDENCE, KINDNESS, LOVE, AND MORE. THEY CANNOT TAKE THESE QUALITIES FROM YOU. KEEP YOUR HEAD UP! GOD LOVES YOU AND HAS GREAT PLANS FOR YOUR LIFE! WE LOVE YOU, SWEET GIRL.

I held that note to my heart as I hid in the girls' bathroom one day during lunch, Libb by my side like always, drying my tears.

My old friends were relentless. They spread rumors up and down the lunch table. They slammed my locker door shut as they passed. They tried breaking Libby and me apart. During my junior year, they laughed when I struggled to open doors as I crutched around school with a broken foot. They whispered old school-bus rumors about my family history to our classmates through the bookshelves in the library during study hall. Anything went as they tried to bring me down.

And it hurt.

But, even during the hardest of times, Mom always seemed to know exactly what to write on the notes in my lunchbox to get me through.

"Though I walk in the midst of trouble, you preserve me against the wrath of my enemies; you stretch out your hand, and your right hand delivers me."

Psalm 138:7

Rachel, keep your faith and hope in God's plan for you. Don't let the girls' jealousy and lies hurt your heart!

Her notes helped me swallow my sandwiches instead of fleeing from the cafeteria.

"... Remember, I am with you always, to the end of the age."

Matthew 28:20

Rachel, no matter what trials we face, christ never leaves us. He is with us every step of the way. even when we feel alone! You are so loved.

Mom had written me thousands of notes over the years, but day after day through high school I'd find:

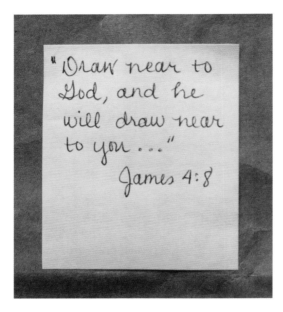

taped to the inside of my lunchbox. She shared that verse of Scripture until the words fit me like a little black dress—perfectly.

The nearer I grew to God as I put my faith in His plan, the wider my wingspan became, and the higher I soared above my old friends. I couldn't believe what had happened to the girls I once loved like sisters, but now even their biggest bullystorms couldn't rain on my parade.

Mom's notes, my best wellies and raincoats, had strengthened me from the inside out, and created resilience that was unbreakable.

The lessons she shared on each note taught me that what I had inside—my faith in God, dreams, talents, strength, passion, positivity, kindness, and confidence—was untouchable. And she was right!

Everything the mean girls did—the bullying, isolation, and rumors—may have challenged my values, but through it all, I stayed true to myself, I kept my faith, and God brought me out stronger than I ever was before. Mom's frequent note of Scripture,

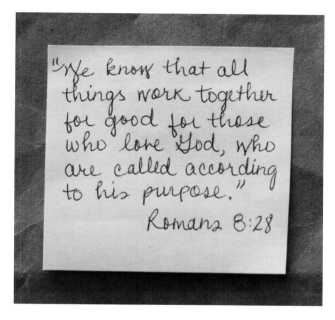

couldn't have been more true. God really did have a bigger plan for me all along. So did Mom.

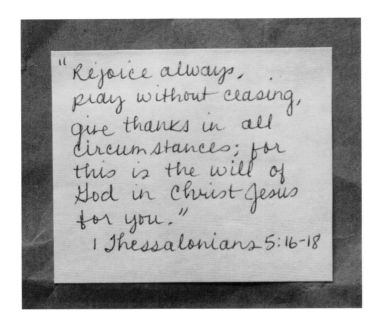

"Rejoice always,
pray without ceasing,
give thanks in all
circumstances; for
this is the will of
God in Christ Jesus
for you."
1 Thessalonians 5:16-18

was a verse of Scripture I found frequently in my lunchbox. I often wondered how I could possibly give thanks in the midst of being bullied, but after years of my mom encouraging me to give thanks even during challenge, I could see why she shared this verse with me so often.

She knew God could use my challenges and hurts for good. As I look back now, I can see that He sure has—and when I expressed gratitude, even in the hardest of times, and lived every day with a hopeful spirit, I was able to spread my wings and fly.

Mom's notes, and my parent's love, helped me bloom right where God had planted me, through the bullystorms and all. And, as I lifted my yellow lunchbox lid one last time on the final day of my senior year, I saw nothing but blue skies ahead.

"SO LET US NOT GROW WEARY IN DOING WHAT IS RIGHT, FOR WE WILL REAP AT HARVEST TIME, IF WE DO NOT GIVE UP."

GALATIANS 6:9

RACHEL, YOU HAVE SHOWN THAT YOU HAVE THE COURAGE TO TRAVEL THE PATH OF LIFE WITH INTEGRITY. YOU HELD TRUE TO THE PROMISE YOU MADE, CHOSE RIGHT OVER WRONG, AND SHOWED KINDNESS AND LOVE TO ALL ON YOUR JOURNEY. WE ARE PROUD OF YOU. WONDERFULLY MADE, BEAUTIFUL INSIDE AND OUT, YOU ARE A TREASURE.

WE LOVE YOU, MOM AND DAD

every good gift
and every perfect
gift is from above
and comes down
from the father of
lights...
    James 1:17

rachel,
thank God for all
the good people
in your life.
    You are loved

We know that all things work
together for good for those who
love God, who are called
according to his purpose.
    Romans 8:28

RACHEL,
YOU HAVE SHOWN THAT YOU HAVE
THE COURAGE TO TRAVEL THE PATH
OF LIFE WITH INTEGRITY. YOU HELD
TRUE TO "THE PROMISE," CHOSE
RIGHT OVER WRONG AND SHOWED
KINDNESS AND LOVE TO ALL ON YOUR
JOURNEY... WE ARE PROUD OF YOU.
WONDERFULLY MADE, BEAUTIFUL
INSIDE AND OUT, YOU ARE A
TREASURE♡ WE LOVE YOU, MOM & DAD

Trust in the Lord with all your
heart, on your own intelligence
rely not; in all your ways be
mindful of him and he will
make straight your path.
    Proverbs 3:5-6

BUT AS FOR ME, I WILL LOOK TO
THE LORD, I WILL WAIT FOR THE
GOD OF MY SALVATION; MY GOD WILL
HEAR ME.   MICAH 7:7
*REMEMBER WHO YOU ARE AND HOW POWERFUL
GOD IS!
FOR THE EYES OF THE LORD RANGE
THROUGHOUT THE ENTIRE EARTH, TO
STRENGTHEN THOSE WHOSE HEART IS
TRUE TO HIM. 2 CHRONICLES 16:9

Have no anxiety at all but in everything by prayer and petition with thanksgiving, make your requests be made known to God, And the peace of God, which surpasses all understanding, will guard your hearts and your minds in Christ Jesus.
Philippians 4:6-7
I prayed for you today ♡

I am going to send an angel before you to guard you along the way... Be on your guard before him and obey his voice...
Exodus 23:20-21

Rachel, Onward & Upward!
. Knowing that suffering produces endurance and endurance produces character, and character produces hope, and hope does not disappoint us because God's love has been poured into our hearts through the Holy Spirit that has been given to us ♡
~ Romans 5:3-5

Our steps are made firm by the Lord, when he delights in our way; though we stumble, we shall not fall headlong, for the Lord holds us by the hand.
Psalm 37:23-24

God indeed is my savior;
I am confident and unafraid. My strength and my courage is the Lord, and he has been my savior.
Isaiah 12:2

From My Lunchbox
To Yours...

From My Lunchbox to Yours . . .

Libby and I stood hand-in-hand on graduation day, our gold rings sparkling on our fingers, our friendship stronger than ever. We had made it, and we continued to soar like the graduation caps we threw into the warm summer air.

Long, carefree sunny days and beautiful sunsets held us sweetly, and as the leaves began to change, I packed up my well-loved, tattered collection of Mom's notes to take with me to college. I had saved each note in a box beneath my bed, and I couldn't help but smile as I read them one by one.

I was in awe of the love my mom had poured into her every word; I could once again feel her love jump off of the note and into my heart like it had every day at school. Each note told a piece of my story, and was special in its own way, but there was one little note from my freshman year that brought me to tears.

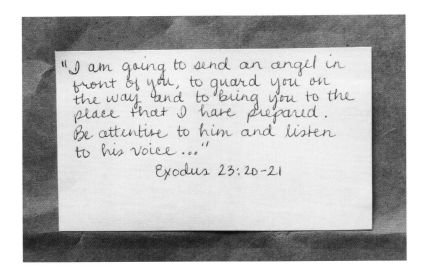

"I am going to send an angel in front of you, to guard you on the way and to bring you to the place that I have prepared. Be attentive to him and listen to his voice ..."

Exodus 23: 20-21

Tears streamed down my cheeks and my vision blurred as I read God's promise.

I knew who that angel was.

Throughout the years, God used many angels to help me persevere through the storm, but there was one angel unlike the rest.

That angel was my mom.

God blessed me with a beautiful, selfless mom who lifted me up every day for thirteen years with the notes she put in my lunchbox. The popularity contests, rumors, bullystorms, and peer pressures of high school could've blown me up, up, and away, but her notes kept me rooted in God's love and my parents' love, built resilience, helped me bloom where God had planted me, and guided me each and every day.

They still guide me!

Her lunchbox notes and the verses from Scripture that she shared created a foundation for my life, and taught me important lessons along the way that empowered me to:

Draw near to God and trust that He had great plans for me.

Express gratitude for all the blessings God put in my life.

Give thanks even during challenge.

Believe that God can use even the hardest moments for good.

Work hard at what I loved to do.

Believe in myself.

Pursue my dreams no matter who tried to get in my way.

Surround myself with loving, supportive friends.

Make the right decisions for me—even if that meant not following the crowd.

Find the good in each day.

Forgive.

Always be kind.

Help others achieve their dreams.

Bloom where I was planted.

Even when the wind was whirling, the hail was hard, and the rain was coming from all directions, I had the strength to persevere through the storm and keep my sunshine thanks to Mom's notes in my lunchbox. And you can help your loved ones do the same!

As they were for me, I hope that these notes will be to you—or someone you love— wellies, raincoats, umbrellas, and most importantly, hope and encouragement for weathering the storms of life.

Here's to blooming right where you've been planted and turning life's storms into sunshine.

From my lunchbox to yours . . . with love.

A Note
From Mom
Written By
Cheri Chadima

A Note from Mom

Cheri Chadima

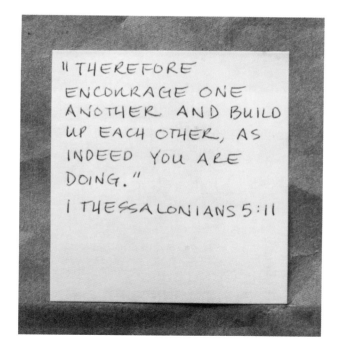

"THEREFORE ENCOURAGE ONE ANOTHER AND BUILD UP EACH OTHER, AS INDEED YOU ARE DOING."

I THESSALONIANS 5:11

When it came time for Rachel to get on the bus to kindergarten, I was so happy for her. On the one hand, there were new friendships that would be formed, caring teachers she would meet, learning she would do, and fun she would have. But, on the other, there was a bit of uncertainty about this whole new world. Just how would she handle school and the challenges of growing up?

Originally, my notes were all about building Rachel's confidence and reminding her that she was loved—big time! I also wanted to plant seeds of faith in her heart so that she would know God more deeply and put her faith and hope in him. I wanted her to know that she was always in my thoughts and loved—*so* much—and that I was praying for her each and every day.

I looked forward to writing notes for Rachel's lunchbox, and it became my way of connecting with her directly during the schooldays. After reading the Bible in my morning devotions, I wrote these notes with love and shared God's promises through the verses that had spoken to me. I felt an assurance that this was the right thing to do. I was confident there was power in my notes and the verses from Scripture, which would give Rachel strength, hope, and a strong biblical foundation. It was my goal to inspire Rachel to be the best person she could be.

As she grew, and when it started to become apparent that Rachel was dealing with mean girls and bullying, it became my mission to help Rachel thrive despite the bullies. I believed and held to my vision for my daughter's success, and I placed my trust in God to act. And, He did.

As I stayed faithful, with a hopeful spirit and my eyes wide open, I witnessed how God worked in Rachel's life as she pressed on with courage and excellence. In those years, many new people and opportunities were brought to her, seemingly at just the right time—angels who showed her she was loved and valued in many different ways. My vision for her success was realized as she soared and grew into a confident, capable, honest young lady with grace and integrity. She excelled in her studies, dance, and personal relationships, as well as anything she put her mind to.

My heart was filled with immense gratitude to God that Rachel had triumphed over the mean girls and bullies. Not only had Rachel been strengthened, but I, too, found that I had been strengthened and my spiritual life had been enriched through reading the Bible and writing her lunchbox notes every day.

Forever grateful, I continue to read God's word in my morning devotions; it is the anchor to my soul. I often share my thoughts and favorite verses with family and friends through a handwritten note or text, for I have seen it have great power.

My heart goes out to anyone who is dealing with mean girls and bullies. I hope you will be inspired by Rachel's story, which is based on her own experiences. It is my prayer that the heartfelt notes and beautiful verses in this book will speak to you and those you love and will bring you strength, courage, and hope.

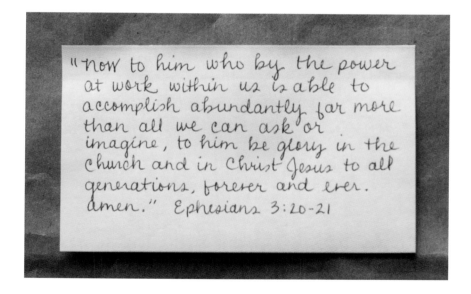

"now to him who by the power at work within us is able to accomplish abundantly far more than all we can ask or imagine, to him be glory in the church and in Christ Jesus to all generations, forever and ever. amen." Ephesians 3:20-21

Lessons for Your Lunchbox

Now, it's your turn!

In this final chapter you'll find notes to share with your loved ones. Whether you use them in their lunchboxes, or use them to inspire the notes you write with your own pen and paper—or even in a noontime text—I hope you find them impactful.

Remember, you can make a difference. *You* can be someone's angel.

lessons for your lunchbox

I feel so lucky that God chose me to be your mom!

I feel so lucky that God chose me to be your dad!

YOU are important to ME

I am proud of you!

We are behind you all the way!

Give thanks for all the blessings in your life!

I praise you because I am fearfully and wonderfully made...
Psalm 139:14
YOU are God's masterpiece!

So in everything, do to others what you would have them do to you...
Matthew 7:12
Treat everyone in your life with kindness, love and respect!

Give thanks to the LORD for he is good; his love endures forever.
Psalm 118:1

...Be strong and courageous. Do not be afraid; do not be discouraged, for the LORD your God will be with you wherever you go.
Joshua 1:9

So do not throw away your confidence; it will be richly rewarded.
Hebrews 10:35
You are one of a kind— stand strong in who you are!

In their hearts humans plan their course, but the LORD establishes their steps.
Proverbs 16:9
Pray big prayers and ask God to show you the way!

You are specially made with talents all your own! Embrace them!

You are here with a purpose. Work hard at what you love to do and lift up others along the way!

Stand out from the crowd—don't be afraid to take the road less traveled!

You can make a difference! Do something sweet for someone today.

Love must be sincere. Hate what is evil; cling to what is good. Romans 12:9

Look to the LORD and his strength; seek his face always. Psalm 105:4

God is our refuge and strength, an ever-present help in trouble. Therefore we will not fear... Psalm 46:1-2

You are beautiful inside and out!

You brighten my day!

I believe in you!

You were made with pure love! God loves you and so do we!

You are a treasure!

Rejoice always, pray continually, give thanks in all circumstances; for this is God's will for you **in Christ Jesus.**
1 Thessalonians 5:16–18
Choose to bloom
where you've been planted!

I am going to send an angel in front of you, to guard you on the way and to bring you to the place that I have prepared. **Be attentive to him and listen to his voice...**
Exodus 23:20–21

Trust in the LORD
with all your heart and lean not on your own understanding; in all your ways acknowledge him, and he will make straight **your paths.**
Proverbs 3:5–6

Therefore I tell you,
whatever you ask for in prayer, believe that you have **received it,** and it will be yours.
Mark 11:24

Therefore encourage one
another and build each other up, just as in fact you are doing.
1 Thessalonians 5:11
Be a cheerleader!

For I am the LORD
your God who takes hold of your right hand and says to you, Do not fear; **I will help you.** Isaiah 41:13

For the eyes of the LORD range throughout the earth to strengthen those whose hearts are fully committed to him...
2 Chronicles 16:9

For I know the plans I have for you, declares the LORD, plans to prosper you and not to harm you, plans to give you hope and a future. Jer 29:11

Let us not get tired of doing what is right, for after awhile we will reap a harvest of blessing if we don't get discouraged and give up.
Galations 6:9

For he will command his angels concerning you to guard you in all your ways.
Psalm 91:11

Do not worry about anything, but in everything by prayer and supplication with thanksgiving let your requests be made known to God.
Philippians 4:6

We know that all things work together for good for those who love God, who are called according to his purpose. Romans 8:28

What is desirable in a person is loyalty.
Proverbs 19:22

You are a joy to be around!

God loves you and so do I!

You are loved ...BIG time!

Draw near to God and he will draw near to you.
James 4:8

I love spending time with YOU!

I will instruct you and teach you in the way you should go; I will counsel you with my loving eye on you. Psalm 32:8

Do not be conformed to this world, but be transformed by the renewing of your minds, so that you may discern what is the will of God—what is good, and acceptable, and perfect. Romans 12:2

...Whenever you face trials of any kind, consider it nothing but joy, because you know that the testing of your faith produces endurance; and let endurance have its full effect, so that you may be mature and complete, lacking in nothing. James 1:2–4

God has big plans—
place your hope and trust in him!

Be strong and courageous. Do not be afraid or terrified because of them, for the LORD your God goes with you; he will never leave you nor forsake you. Deuteronomy 31:6

Surely God is my salvation; I will trust and not be afraid. The LORD is my strength and my defense... Isaiah 12:2

I know that you are pleased with me, for my enemy does not triumph over me. Because of my integrity you uphold me and set me in your presence forever. Psalm 41:11–12

Some friends play at friendship, but a true friend sticks closer than one's nearest kin. Proverbs 18:24

You are the star in our eyes... kind, loving, intelligent and beautiful inside and out. You amaze us!

But as for me, I will look to the LORD, I will wait for the God of my salvation; my God will hear me. Micah 7:7

...Let your light shine before others, so that they may see your good works and give glory to your father in heaven. Matthew 5:16

Let go of anything negative. Look forward with strength, optimism, energy, and hope! You are loved!

Now faith is confidence in what we hope for and assurance about what we do not see. Heb 11:1

Believe and you will **succeed!** Dream BIG!

You are a joy to be around!

Cast all your anxiety on him because he cares for you. 1 Pet 5:7

You can do anything you put your mind to!!

Live life with an attitude of gratitude!

You are my perfect gift from God!

You
are such a
hard worker!

Life is grand!
What are you
grateful
for today?

Be kind
to one another.
-Ellen DeGeneres

I trust you
to make
great
decisions!

You will
never regret
being kind!

Your smile
lights up
a room!

Believe
in your dreams...
YOU CAN
achieve them!

You are wonderfully made
—unlike anyone else.
Embrace
your unique qualities!

Thinking
of you
with a smile!

**Ask,
Believe,**
and Receive!

**Choose an attitude
of enthusiasm!
Shine bright
and live life
to the fullest!**

Chase your dreams!
**We're cheering
you on!**

A friend loves at all times, and kinsfolk are born to share adversity.
Proverbs 17:17

Move through the day with hope, confidence, and gratitude. You've got this!

Do the very best you can -always!

For truly I tell you, if you have faith the size of a mustard seed, you will say 'Move from here to there,' to this mountain, and it will move; and nothing will be impossible for you.
Matthew 17:20

Smile, you are loved and so special to me.

God has you in the palm of his hand!

Put your trust in God's plan for your life!

Be a blessing to someone today! We rise in lifting others!

Keep God 1st place in your life!

Trust in God! He has great plans for you!

Be still and know that he is God.
Psalm 46:10

I can do all things through him who strengthens me.
Philippians 4:13

Listen to your heart
and what makes it glad.
What gives you joy?
You give me joy!

I can do all things
through him
who strengthens me.
Philippians 4:13

About The
Author

About the Author

Born and raised in the wide-open spaces, Rachel is a lover of her roots with a love for fashion, writing, travel, fitness, and her Christian faith. She finds great joy in belly laughs with her girlfriends, a glass of good red wine, finding that perfect verse of Scripture for the moment, a butt-kicking workout, cheering on the Minnesota Wild, spending time with her parents on the farm she's loved since dress-up days and chores with dad, a warm latte, jet-setting with her husband, big family dinners, and country music.